# THE Tim March BMX BOOK

# THE *Tim March* BMX BOOK

HAMLYN

**Photographic acknowledgments**
All photographs by David Spurdens except
p. 14 (Ammaco BMX Ltd), p. 20 (Motor Sport Photos),
p. 21 top (Ammaco BMX Ltd), p. 28 middle
(Ammaco BMX Ltd)

Published 1985 by
Hamlyn Publishing
Bridge House, London Road,
Twickenham, Middlesex

ISBN 0 600 50193 0

Phototypeset by Photocomp Ltd, Birmingham
Printed in Italy

# CONTENTS

# WHERE IT STARTED

BMX as a sport grew out of Motocross of the motorbike variety. So many of the original BMXers started with Motocross, and I was one of the first to make that journey. The advantages are obvious in taking up BMX rather than Motocross. Firstly, there is the expense. You can get your BMX bike to local meetings and compete and, of course, you can buy it in the first place much more easily and cheaply.

I was 14 years old when I managed to convince my dad to buy me a motorbike. It was only a cheap old thing but it started the ball rolling for me in wheel sports.

I entered the world of Motocross by getting to a few small meetings and gradually crept up through the ranks in schoolboy Motocross. When I was 17 I started to compete in adult Motocross. All along I had managed to obtain some sponsorship from firms such as KPM and Honda, but in adult Motocross I found it very difficult to afford the sport with the expense of the upkeep of my bike, buying spare parts and travelling to meetings all over the UK. One of the big problems with the motorbike branch of the sport is the speed with which parts wear out. It became so much of a struggle that at the age of 19 I decided to change to BMX.

*Right above:* I wouldn't want so much air in a race unless I had it sewn up.

*Right:* It's me coming down on the earth's side of a moondrop!

*Centre:* Most of the time I have my feet firmly on the ground, but I can hit the airwaves when I have to!

# FOR TIM MARCH

**Top:** Me!

**Above:** Here I'm getting gnarly and intense; you have to do these things to forge the understanding between man and his machine.

I had heard a lot about it, because the two sports are pretty similar in many ways, and BMX appealed to me a great deal.

One of the things that really attracted me was the fact that the rider is the only source of propulsion. There is no engine. *You* are the engine and you can't go out and buy a more powerful one if you aren't doing very well; you have to get out there and train and work a lot harder if you want to be successful.

I was introduced to BMX by the Americans. One year I went to the USA on holiday with a couple of Motocross friends, and I saw a BMX race over there at Ascot; when I came back I went straight to my local bike shop to get a BMX bike, a Mongoose.

I couldn't wait! I had been bitten by the BMX bug and I started racing immediately the bike was delivered.

At that time BMX racing wasn't properly organized in the UK. It was just a case of riding round the streets or on any waste ground you could find. I had to wait six months for a proper race meeting, and it took place at a track in Kent called Buckmoor Park.

I raced in the 16 expert age group, even though I was 19, but in those days the 16s was the oldest age group. Now it's 17+. I won all my heats there and clinched the final so I reckoned I was cut out for the sport!

 Quite a number of the riders I now compete against on the professional circuit were at that meeting and are still my greatest opponents— riders such as Andy Ruffell and Pete Middleton. They had probably been taking part in BMX longer than I had, but I seemed to take to it naturally.

However, it soon became clear that it wasn't going to be any easier financing myself properly at BMX than it was to keep going in Motocross, so I decided to sell the BMX bike and give motorbikes another chance. No sooner had I done that than an opportunity presented itself that I couldn't ignore. What happened was that Ammaco, who were marketing Mongoose products in the UK, made it known that they wanted riders for their team. I contacted them and offered to ride and become a representative for them, selling their products to shops and wholesalers. They took me on and in that first year, 1982, I managed to get a UK number 1 plate. In the same year I had improved to the point where

*The Mongoose bike – the same make with which I started.*

*Part of being a BMX star is PR work and mixing with the people.*

was born. In this year, 1984, March products spread from a range of three or four to sixteen BMX lines, and March Racing was formed.

I knew who I wanted in my team right at the start so I went after them to see if they were interested. Frankie Romain, Anthony Howells and little Colin Webb were the main names and by the beginning of the 1984 season I had put together a full team. Amazingly, it was good enough to win the UK team trophy for the season, and we had a great time doing it! In 1984 I dropped Cruiser but made No. 1 spot for the 20 in. class in the UK and Europe. I also went to the World Championships in Japan, and they were to prove one of the most frustrating occasions of my career.

I went really well in the motos, and the final was a three-leg event just like the Pro finals in the UK. I won all three mains but then disaster struck. An American judge

disqualified me for dangerous riding! I couldn't believe it. I had ridden hard and aggressively—you have to in a World Championship, otherwise you end up with the wooden spoon—but I certainly don't think I rode dirtily. I still reckon, even now, that I should be World Champion; but we have to have officials otherwise the sport would be a free-for-all, and I am subject to their rulings just like anyone else!

I was able to beat Harry Leary in the Anglo-American meeting held at Redditch, which was a real boost.

I didn't stay with Ammaco very long, and I soon joined Geoff Barraclough at G.T. for the 1983 season; it was at this time that I started my business of manufacturing BMX products. It was a small concern, and you can't get much smaller than making race plates on the table and floor of your mum's kitchen! Still, it went well; I was manufacturer, marketing manager and salesman all in one, but the main thing was that *my* plates were getting into the important dealers and wholesalers. 1983 was a fantastic season for me and the best confirmation I could have had that I had made the right decision in moving from motorbikes to BMX. I managed to gain the UK 20 in. and Cruiser No. 1 spots, and the European 20 in. and Cruiser crowns. In the same year I won the big UK meeting at Pickets Lock, which was sponsored by Lee Cooper, and it was after this that I received their sponsorship.

The following year proved to be just as successful for me. Tran-Am became interested in my products and we completed a deal. M.R.D.

*Dig the barnet. The smile was inspired by that piece of paper in my left hand!*

*Opposite:* I will land on my rear wheel and push the front down after landing—looks good doesn't it?!

*Below:* This is me in between sponsors and just after my Mongoose period.

# THE BMX RACER

BMX must surely be one of the best popular sports to emerge in the past 100 years. The first step to becoming a BMX racer is quite obviously to buy a BMX bike. It doesn't really matter how much you pay for it, or how good it is. Once you are in possession of it you are a member of the society, although you have a long way to progress before you become an honorary member.

It doesn't matter whether you have an expensive or a cheaper bike, you can still race. You may not do as well on a cheaper bike, but you can start to make a name for yourself at a club by doing well on race days. Most importantly, you can set about gaining experience.

## Trackcraft

This is a magic word in BMX and all the good riders have it. However, they didn't gain it just like that. They had to work at it for many hours, and watch other riders who had been racing longer than they had, in order to pick up tips on how to improve. Joining your local club is a good step to making this beginning. Today young BMXers are fortunate because there are tracks in all major districts, and plenty are being constructed in rural and outlying areas.

Nearly all clubs have practice nights, and it is at these that you must build up your confidence and skill ready for that magical first race.

Your first race will usually be a club race, which means you will be competing only against riders from your own club. This is the best one to kick off with. There is nothing worse than to start off at too high a level and get thoroughly trounced. It won't do a lot for your confidence.

**Top:** A region's qualifiers for the Champion of Champions meeting.

**Above:** The fraternity.

16

The club structure is well organized in the UK because it does allow you to progress in stages: the next step in racing is to ride in a club Open meeting. This will be run by your club and will have most of your club members competing, but there will also be riders from other clubs in your area. This way you can broaden your experience gradually, and you should be improving all the time.

Your club will be part of a BMX region, usually comprising a number of clubs, and the next rung up after the club Open meeting is the Regional.

The Regionals are a great step towards making a name for yourself, because they can lead to National Championships—more about these later. There are 11 regions in the UK as far as the UKBMX Association is concerned, and each year they select champions to represent them at a National venue called the Champion of Champions.

The other association controlling BMX in the UK is the NBMXA, who also run a Regional championship climaxing in a National one called the British Championship.

The Regionals are run over a period of time, and usually at the major tracks in the area, and the first eight in each age group go forward to the National venues. If you have worked hard at your club and have carried out the necessary training, you have a good chance of getting into the best eight in your area, and that means your first taste of the National scene and all the excitement it brings with it.

The razamatazz at a National/Regional meeting is amazing; it has

**Top:** *The club meeting—a good place to start.*

**Above:** *Club focus.*

*Left:* Wayne Llewelyn,
14 year old
superstar and
European number 1.

*Above:* Gary Llewelyn, older brother of Wayne, and making his way to the European Superclass crown.

*Right:* John Vile, number 1 UKBMX in 1984 and going Superclass now; he's fast!

to be seen to be believed. The Nationals/Regionals are always held at a big arena such as Olympia. All the regions turn out in force and the chanting and cheering of thousands of fans ensures an electric atmosphere by the time the finals take place.

## The Nationals

The next step up the rung of the BMX staircase is the National. This is the meeting where you will ride for your National plate, and where you will have to compete against the best riders in the country; and, of course, you will be riding on the best tracks in the country too.

Once again the two BMX associations have their own National set-up, venues and ratings. You can compete in both if you have the time and the money, and many riders do exactly that.

Since the Nationals started in 1980 there have been varying numbers of them, but now they seem to have settled for about nine per year and these are held all round the UK. This is one of the reasons why, once you have reached this level, you need either a private source of finance or a sponsor or two.

The riders who can compete in all the Nationals usually have sponsorship from a team (see the chapter on the BMX team), a manufacturer or distributor, or a shop. If you have been making a name for yourself on the way up to the Nationals you will probably have got a few of these people interested in your ability and this will help to finance the operation for you.

*Above:* NBMXA North West Winter Series 1984–85; all the class winners with Andy Ruffell, who presented the trophies.

There can be 1000+ riders at a National, and the structure in the UK is that all the races take place on the same day. As you can imagine, that is one very hectic occasion, and you will be 'on the go' from the minute you arrive till the minute you go home or drop out of the reckoning. Dropping out of the reckoning means that you have not qualified for the next stage of the competition.

The first stage of the National consists of the three motos (heats). These will take place in your age group or class. You will only have three of these, but there may well be a number of them in your age group. Usually you will qualify for the next stage if you can get around the twelve points mark, and the points are awarded according to the position you achieve in each moto, e.g. if you come fourth three times you get twelve points. If you come sixth in two of your motos, even a first in the last one might mean that your day is finished! This isn't always so, and in a large sign-up you might well get through to the next round on that performance.

Whether you have qualifying rounds or not will depend on the number of riders of your age. The qualifiers will be held to whittle

*Opposite top:* BMX at Olympia.

*Opposite below:* Wild antics at the bottom of the start hill.

down the competitors to a sensible number so that semi-finals can be run and then, of course, a final. You might, for example, have sixteenths, eighths, quarters and then semis. From the moment you go into qualifiers it is the first four home in each race that go through to the next qualifier. You should see the excitement these qualifiers generate, especially in the battle over who gets that 'golden' fourth place!

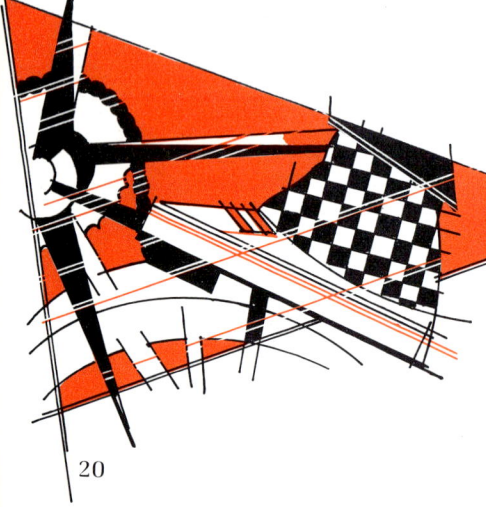

At a large meeting you can imagine how the tension builds up when a rider has pulled himself through all these heats and has reached the semi-final. The noise from the spectators is deafening and the riders go for maximum speed and take risks now that the final goal is close.

Once a rider has reached the final he has everything to ride for and nothing to lose. Already he has earned points towards his National plate, and if he can get a good position in the final his rating will go up even more.

The experienced riders know the individual tracks and they also know the significance of the lane draw. For the final it is drawn with the use of pegs up on the start hill,

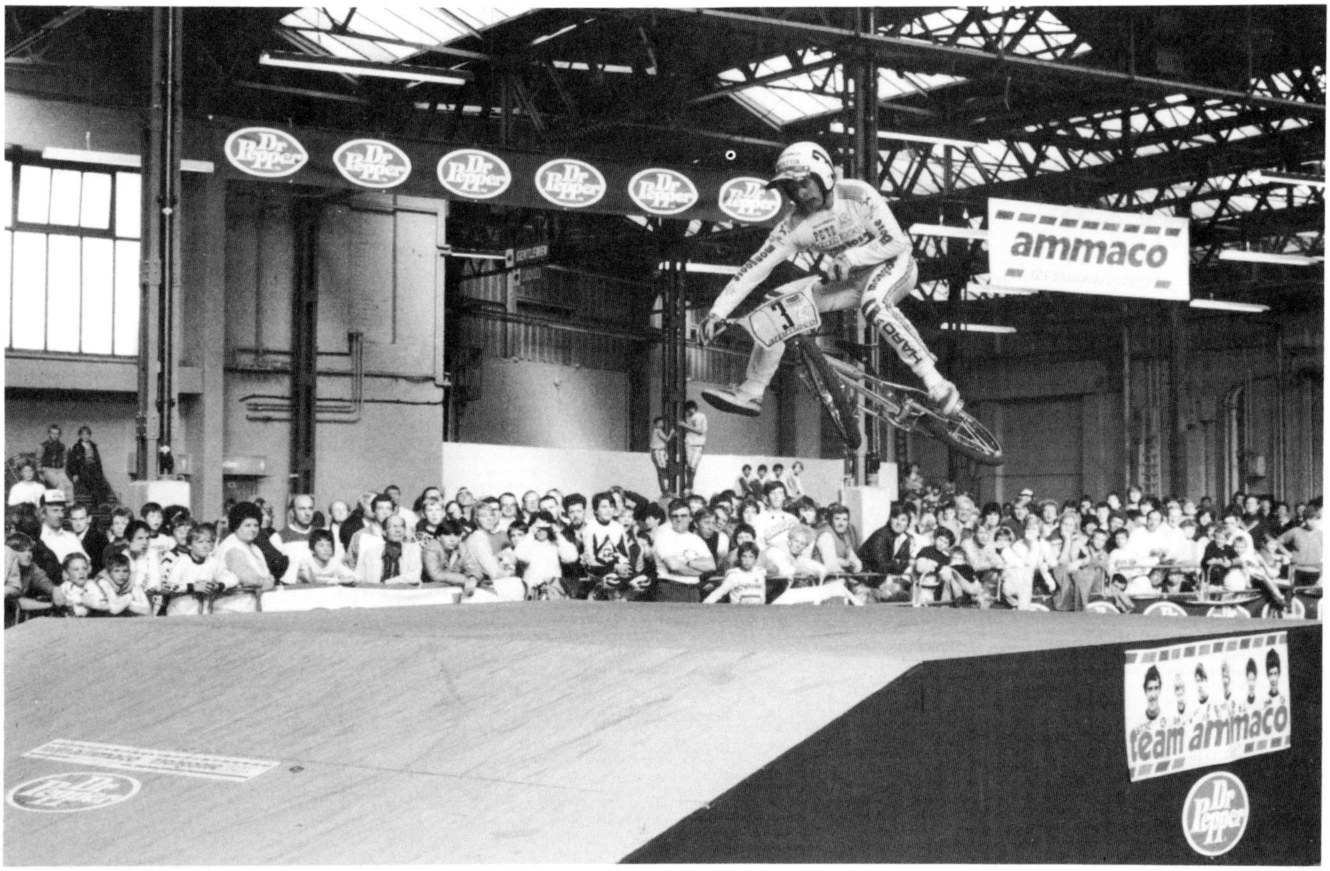
Dr Pepper
ammaco
team ammaco

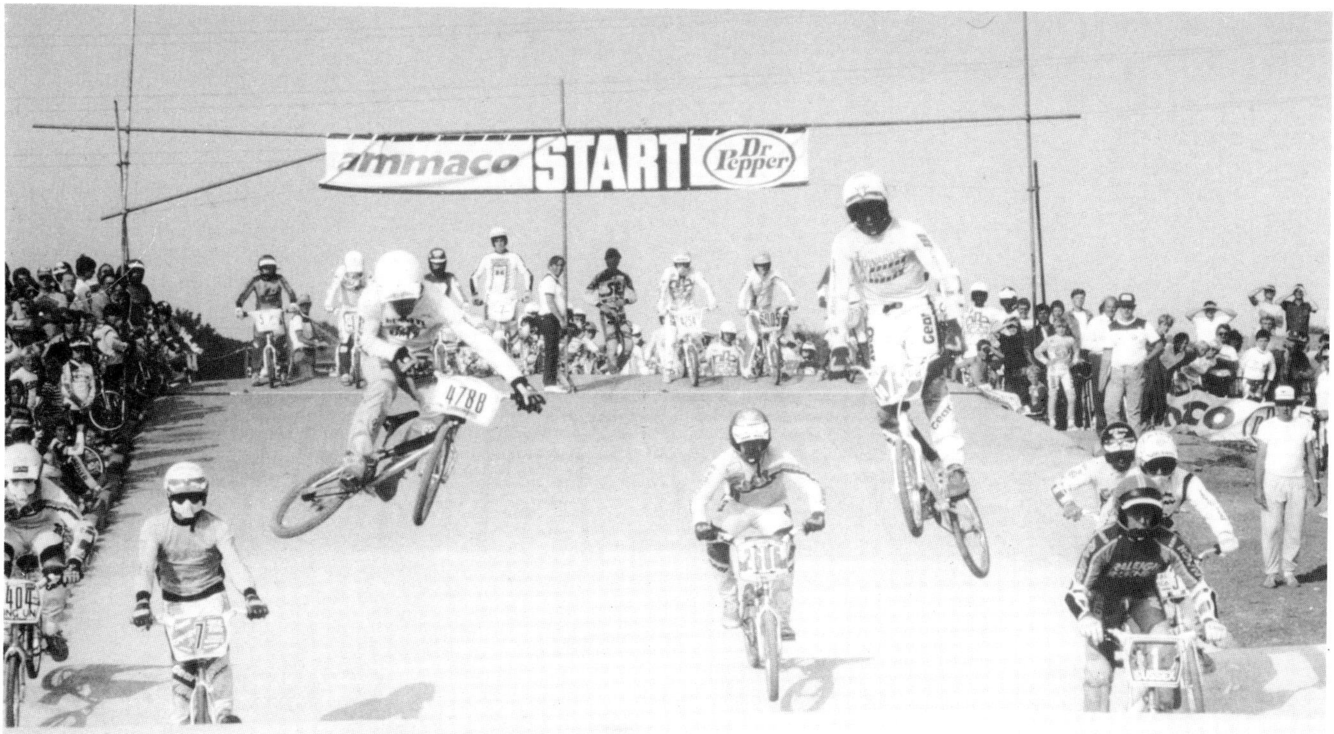
ammaco START Dr Pepper
4788

and from the moment the lanes are allocated the riders know whether they have increased or decreased their chances with the lane they have drawn. They also know what sort of a race they must ride, for example, whether the start is now all-important or whether tactics will do it for them when they come to the berms (bends). A good rider will be thinking about tactics from the moment he learns he is in the final, and will be considering the tactics he knows or thinks his opponents will adopt.

## The National final

This is a mind-boggling occasion, especially when it has been reached through so many qualifiers. To be in the last eight when there have been 1200 riders competing at National level is a great achievement.

The scoring system at National finals gives fifteen points to the winner, twelve to the second rider, ten for the third then a fall of one point for each rider down to the last home. Points are allocated to riders once they get to a semi. Waiting for your final seems to take an age and any hold-ups for crashes or other reasons can put up your heart rate dramatically. It helps in winning finals if you have a big-race temperament, and that means thinking positively about how you are going to ride. Your concentration on the start hill has to be 100%!

Whether it is a manual or an electric start (not many of these exist in the UK at present) you have to make sure your whole body and mind are geared to instant response once the start signal has been given.

*You're off!* You know immediately whether you have had a dream start or have blown it at the gate. You also know, if you haven't got out first, whether you can pull back the deficit. Whichever way it's gone, you know that you have to move like a bat out of hell now. It's all or nothing! You are not conscious of the crowd or anything else, but just your opponents and the track.

You squeeze every last grain of energy and concentration out of yourself until you reach the finish line. Have you won? Great if you have but it's a big achievement anyway, even if you have come last, to have reached the final. Great too if you went out in the motos. At least you have been part of the great BMX action show and the next meeting could be different; perhaps then you will make the final. One thing's for sure: if you haven't done

well at this one, it ought to make you work a bit harder to make sure you do better at the next!

**Top:** *MRD's Superclass rider Frankie Romain putting on the style; a great character, Frankie, and well liked on the circuit.*

**Above:** *It's me, but that flyer Geth Shooter is giving me hassle again.*

*In the JMC gear, Rachel Holmes, one of the UK's top girls.*

23

# THE BMX BIKE

The BMX bike is a wonderful machine. Never in the history of cycling has such a fantastic machine been manufactured that allows its owner such a broad spectrum of activity! It can be ridden, it can fly; it can do somersaults, spin, turn jump, land and generally perform such an awesome range of movement that one wonders whether its designer came from where E.T. went!

Just consider some of the jumps it has to contend with when next you are at a track. Look at the 'air' some of the riders get, the speeds they reach and the way they negotiate the most difficult obstacles, and you will agree that the BMX bike has to take its place among some of the most ingenious inventions! OK, enough of this. If you already have a BMX bike you know all this anyway, and if you haven't, then you know you have to buy one!

*Below: A unique bike made in France: it is actually glued together. Peugeot market it for about £250.*

*Above: A real oddball bike and one causing a bit of controversy. The hawser wire is tensioned by bolts under the bottom bracket and UKBMX are not happy about the dangers it might present.*

## Choosing the bike for you

Two factors dominate your decision on which bike is for you: money and the level of competition at which you are. Let us look at money first, since without it you are not going to have to worry about the other anyway!

If you are taking BMX seriously but coming in at the ground floor, then you don't want to spend more than necessary with the very good chance that once you get started you may have made the wrong decision.

Let's get it straight before we proceed: you are not going to make much of a reputation for yourself in good company if you buy a real cheapie under the £70 mark. Go above £100 and you're getting somewhere. What is the difference between a bike under £70 and one that costs a little more than £100?

Well for a start you can bet your 'cheapie' will be very heavy and it will be hung with poor

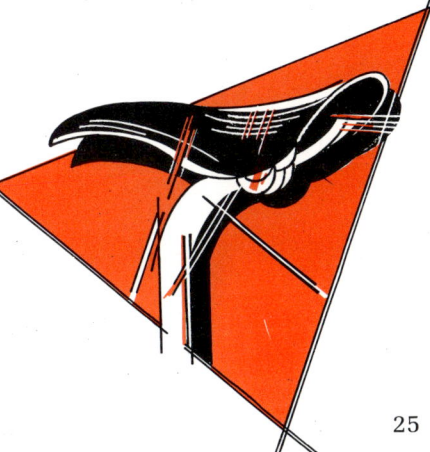

componentry. It won't matter how good you are, you'll struggle on this one. It will be made of steel as will all the components. The welding won't be all that good and you will probably find that the first heavy landing will see you back at the shop complaining that you have cracked one of the joints. The next step up from a machine of this calibre is to get a frame which is made of T4130 chrome–moly.

This is a different ball game. It is stronger than mild steel and allows the gauge used for the frame and the forks to be thinner, and this is where the weight saving is made. These T4130 frame and forks usually have some smart TIG (tungsten inert gas) welding on them and are quite a strong unit.

Look around and make sure you are getting value for money. You can pay the same price for a mild steel bike and it will certainly be heavier. The frame and forks need to be strong and they need to be

light, or as light as you can get them, but after that you want to look at the design. The engine room of a bike is the bottom bracket, and its relationship with the crank and the freewheel.

First of all let us look at the position of the bottom bracket. Check it to make sure you are not going to have trouble with it being too low for the pedal cranks you are going to use. This is very important if you are a bigger rider and you want to use 180 mm cranks. You may not be able to go for the bike which has the shorter triangle at the back (the triangle formed between the chain stays, the seat stays and the seat post). These bikes have a lower bottom bracket mostly, whereas the longer frame hangs the cranks higher.

Here is why you want to check this carefully: the short triangle

*The biker's dream world— hundreds of bikes and trick bits to choose from.*

gives you greater more-immediate power out of the gate and has a quicker response to the demands of the BMX obstacle course. If you are a smaller rider you would be better off going for this type of bike. However, if you are a big dude you will want to find the happy medium, which means only going as long as you are forced to!

While we're on bottom brackets a word on what to expect in the way of cranks on your £100+ bike. For sure you are going to have to settle for a one-piece and, unless you are very lucky, it will be mild steel. You might find one with chrome – moly cranks and, if you can, you will have made a weight saving in this department. Usually you find that you have to be looking at the £150+ market to get this componentry as part of the package.

Before we go any further, always remember you can update your componentry as you go along, and you might find it well worthwhile looking at the second-hand market for your modifications.

Your spider and chainwheel will be of mild steel and so will the rest of the componentry. This means you are probably looking at a finished bike with an overall weight of 25–28 lb. You can race with that and do very well. Further up-market, and for a complete bike costing £200, you can get a great improvement in the componentry and you will be looking at a frame and forks made from T4130 chrome–moly.

*Right:* When it comes to unusual bikes and wild things happening on them, the phenomenon of the Pit bike takes some beating. It's a very small bike with 14 in. wheels and you'd be amazed at the things you can do on it.

*Opposite left:* A power wheelie over the speed jumps.

*Opposite right:* The Grand Prix: middle range racer and great value for money; you can race on this and win.

*Opposite top:* And here's the bike I can't speak too highly of: the one and only M.R.D. bike in action. This is an English bike and I'll put it against anything on the market.

You are probably wondering what other forms of chrome–moly there are and how they can be superior. Well there are the elite chrome–molys and they are Reynolds 531 tubing and T45 tubing, and these are chromanganese metals which are very strong; for that reason they can be used as a much thinner-gauge tubing, thereby giving the same

strength as steel or T4130 but with less weight.

Back to the £200+ bike, and here you can expect both frame and forks to be made from T4130, whereas the £100+ bike will probably have a frame made from this material and the forks of high tensile steel. You will be looking at aluminium stems and wheels, and possibly a chrome–moly one-piece crank. You might, if you are lucky, get aluminium pedals and a good lightweight brake assembly. Weight-wise you are now getting down under the 25 lb level and could go as low as 23 lb. This gives you every chance on the racing circuits and there are many well known racers who actually forged their reputations on just such a machine!

As in all sports, the people at the top are always looking for the very best equipment they can get hold of. They have proved they have the ability by building their reputations on bikes in the lower and middle-class brackets, but once they are nearing the top it gets tougher, and there are a lot of people just itching to take their place.

Having reached the £200–£250/300 region for their bikes, you might wonder just how much further they can go. The answer is—a lot! If they really want to go for the ultimate in biking luxury they can actually add another £1000 to that figure!

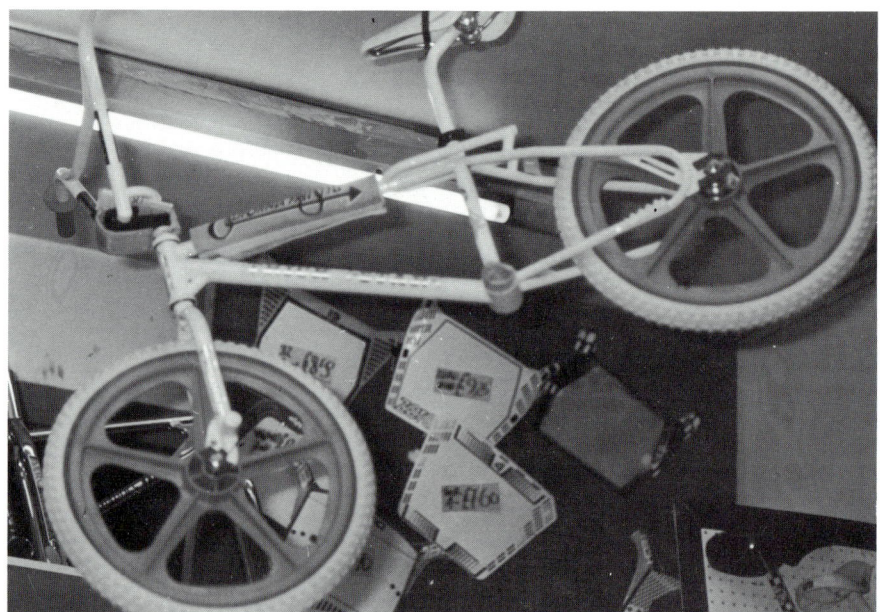

Hutch, the American manufacturer, make a bike which can set you back £1100 and if you go into the Titanium range you can rise to £1300 without trying too hard. Titanium is the wonder metal perfected by the aerospace and car-racing industries, and it allows whole bikes in the Mini or Midi range to come down in weight to 9¾ lb!

The Hutch bike is hung with a dazzling array of componentry, which is what drags the price up to such a high level. It has three-piece cranks which are pure chrome–moly. The bottom bracket, chain wheel and just about every other part on it will be of the same material, and it will make a weight of just under 20 lb for a full-size machine.

## The check-list when buying a bike

**Drop-outs:** These are the bits you will find at the bottom of the front and rear forks and incorporate the axle housings. They are a lot thicker than the actual tubing used for the frame and forks, but make sure they have most of their bulkiness above the axle housing since this is where the stress occurs.

**Seat post angle:** If you are a bigger rider, look for a seat post which moves the position of the seat back and will make the bike more comfortable for you. If you can't find a bike that suits you in this respect, with everything else being satisfactory, then you will have to go for the laid-back seat post.

**Steering:** Different riders prefer different steering responses and the design of the bike plays a big part in deciding this.

The angle of the forks is a major factor and the 'rake' of the forks (the extent to which they project further than an imaginary line through the bar stem and downwards) will determine whether the steering is 'quick response' or 'slow response'. The further the forks project the slower the steering, so the more the forks are tucked under the head tube the quicker the steering. In studying the geometry this is a major factor to be considered in getting the bike that suits your personal likes and dislikes.

*Opposite top:* The C.W. California, an upper middle class freestyler for about £300.

*Opposite centre:* Mongoose Grand Prix, middle range, just under the £200 mark.

*Opposite bottom:* Revolutionary design, or is it? The Rocket actually looks like the Schwinn of early American BMX—a good bike.

*Above:* A D.P. freestyler made by Dave Parks at his factory in Wales: cost?—about £200.

*Left:* The JMC with top componentry; think of about £300+ for this one.

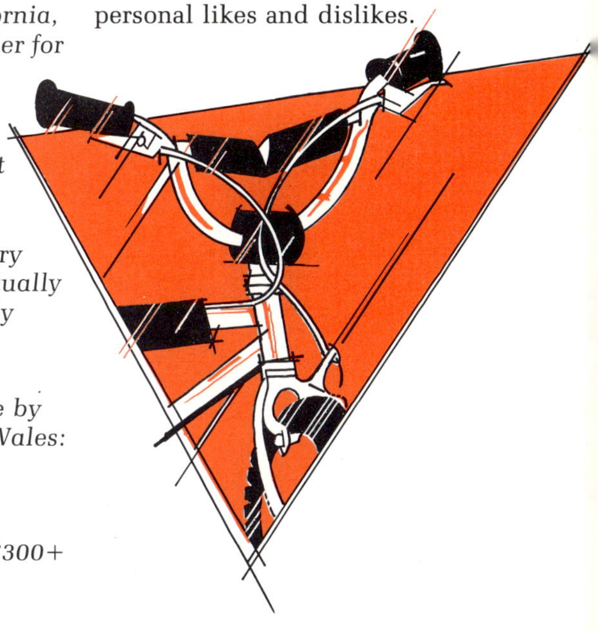

**Top:** The one and only R.L. Osborne showing what the Redline bike can do.

**Above:** The Redline Freestyle bike: slightly up-market and loaded with componentry. £300+ and a great looker, which means a lot to the performer.

**Left:** The Raleigh bike: English made and a great saviour to the British bike industry: on top of that some very radical machines.

# RACING TO WIN

Racing to win and racing to enjoy it are exactly the same thing to me. If you are winning you are enjoying yourself, especially if winning is important to you. The trouble is, not everybody can be number 1. Somebody has to come second, and there are always plenty of other riders who have to come a long way behind that. So how do you arrive at the best attitude to make you get the maximum from your sport?

I think the secret lies in saying, 'You can only ever do your best'. If you follow this maxim you will never let anybody down and that includes yourself. The worst way in which a rider can leave a race meeting is to have to admit to himself that he could have tried a lot harder. If you come last of all the moto riders, but you can go home

**Above:** Perfect speed jumping technique.

**Left:** Nationals have become so big now, they're running into the night. The guy on the deck didn't have his headlights on!

32

saying that you couldn't possibly have tried any harder, then you are going to get a good night's sleep!

No matter what standard you are, there is one thing that is a certainty—you can always get better!

If you work at it you can improve every part of your racing ability and your tactics. You have to work at it and be prepared to listen to people with more experience than you. You have to improve your physical fitness and you have to brush up on your technique. The best way of doing that is to get out there and physically bring about an improvement. The other way you can help yourself to get better is to read about other riders and to watch videos of top racers.

In this section I am going to give you some tips which will, hopefully, make you into a better racer, and that can only lead to you enjoying your sport more. Many riders maintain that if you can be a good gater you are more than

halfway to success. I wouldn't put it that strongly but it is certainly a big part of any racer's success.

Gating is all about balance, concentration, technique and power. The trouble is that you have to combine all these qualities to emerge with the perfect starting technique.

**Top:** *Look at the 5's style: you can see why he's in front!*

**Above:** *Bermology.*

## Balance

Let us look at balance first: you don't need it if you are going for a one-pedal start, but today, most riders are agreed this is an inferior technique. For two-pedal starts you must be poised at the gate with perfect steadiness, and the more relaxed you are in holding the balanced position, the more you will be able to react to the commands and signals that will follow. If you are battling to stay upright there is no way you are going to respond to the lights changing to green or the manual command of, 'Riders ready, Pedals ready, Go!'

Find the crank position that (a) suits your style, and (b) suits your gearing. Remember, the higher the gearing the higher you need to be on your cranks to get that massive downward thrust.

Practise your balances at every opportunity. It is something you can do all the time because the facilities are all around you: a wall, a fence, a block of concrete. These are all potential practice areas for starting balance.

## Bike position

Get your bike lined up straight to the gate. If you have the line of your bike at an angle to the gate you are more likely to get back-wheel spin. Keep the front wheel straight and the line of the bike at perfect right-angles to the gate.

**Opposite and this page:** Frankie being pushed by Long John (Legs) Baldry. The action got too hot for the guy in third.

**Opposite top:** Indoor action from Paris. Note the imported dirt track: they're usually a disaster. We tend to go for wood.

**Top:** Anthony Howells (1) in the lead over the speed jumps

## The starter's cadence or the lights' sequence

Get to know the starter's 'cadence' (his timing or rhythm). Once you are in tune with this, you have the advantage of being able to anticipate the fall of the gate and initiate your final moves up to the 'off'.

The same thing goes when lights are being used. They will have a timing sequence, and the more that is programmed into your reactions the better off you will be. Where lights are being used you have to decide exactly where you are going to look to register the change. I find it best to use the 'peripheral' technique. That is to say, I don't look straight at the lights, but I look at the hill and observe the lights as part of my overall vision. This way I can also take account of movements made by my opponents. Some riders look straight at the lights, but I think this is bad for balance since the head has to be held at an unnatural angle.

## The final push (pelvis to stem)

At the moment you are to fly out of the gate you must thrust your pelvis at the bar stem. Throw your head slightly backwards, pull on your straightened arms and drive for all you are worth.

*Hanging about at the gate can be murder.*

*It's Peter Barnsby (5); he's part of Rainbow Racing now and looking good.*

driving seat—you decide! If you haven't, then you have to take the line that is most likely to improve your position. You may decide to take the lower line and swoop inside the opposition and this is known as the Block Pass. You might prefer to opt though for something just as drastic and go for a swoop from a higher position. This means you go as high as you can on the nearside of the berm and then drop in to the near exit at an acute angle. This is a high-risk move, but it can get you from a 'no hope' position to the front, and only *you* can know whether it's worth it! Another decision you have to make is whether you can increase your speed by using the high rims of the berm, and whether or not it will cost you time in getting to the rims.

## Berm protection techniques

It is legitimate race strategy to use certain techniques to protect a lead when you are riding the berms.

The most common of these is to ride with a spread-elbows style. This means you are cutting down the room on either side of you for other riders to get by. Another popular move is to put a leg down on the side where you think another rider might be coming through.

## Out of the gate

Now you are out of the gate you want to maintain the momentum, and that means the maximum torque by thrusting down on the pedals. For this to happen, you need your weight to be shifted back over the seat and to be working hard with every part of your body.

## The zig-zag problem

There will always be a slight side-to-side movement when you are generating this sort of power, but you must not let it get out of hand. If it becomes emphasized it will deprive you of forward momentum.

## The holeshot

It's the situation every rider wants: to be in front by the time the first berm looms up. It's a great position to be in, but it isn't a guarantee that you are going to hold it if you don't start thinking seriously about your lines now.

Many factors determine the line you will take at the first berm, such as the shape of the track, the shape of the berm, the line you want to take out of the berm and any obstacles you are going to encounter before and after it. The best line is the one that allows you to be pedalling as fast and for as long as you can, and if you have the holeshot you are the man in the

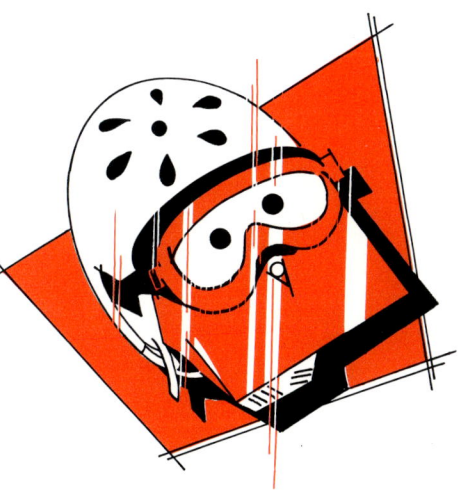

**Left:** Frankie Romain coming into land after a spooky table top.

**Right:** Tim and Frankie speed jumping.

**Right:** Frankie knows what's happening behind him, and he'll take the line that shuts down the most threats.

39

## Speed jumping

I have talked about riding the berms before dealing with the speed jumps, because I wanted to convey the importance of taking the right line, but of course on most tracks you will encounter a speed jump before you come to a berm, and it is important that you have the right technique to deal with this, otherwise you could find yourself at the back by the first bend.

The first technique you need to master to be a perfect speed jumper is the power wheelie. This is the lifting of the front wheel while you are still pedalling, to get the front wheel up and over the face of the jump with minimum impact. It is a superbly stylish move and very practical because it maintains the momentum you have built up at the start.

All the best riders keep pedalling right up to the jumps, and the top men can keep pedalling as they go over them too!

*Opposite top:* Pete Middleton.

*Opposite bottom:* Spectacular air but it doesn't always win races.

*Left:* Front wheel lift where it shouldn't be.

*Below* Low plates, high plates. Everybody is in with a chance.

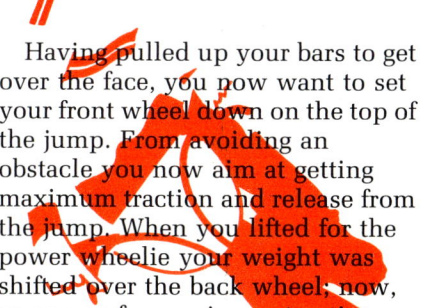

Having pulled up your bars to get over the face, you now want to set your front wheel down on the top of the jump. From avoiding an obstacle you now aim at getting maximum traction and release from the jump. When you lifted for the power wheelie your weight was shifted over the back wheel; now, as you go for maximum traction, you must shift your weight over the seat and drive straight down through the cranks.

*Opposite:* Sitting down isn't advisable when the opposition is close; I must have been near the finish.

*Above:* This is Tony Holland. He's Torker now but still as fast. Relax for a minute and he's the type of rider to put egg on your face!

*Right:* Charlie is a great jumper, but when the chips are down he goes for max. trax!

## Braking

Only use your brakes when you really have to. Don't surrender advantage or give up a challenge by putting on your brakes when you have the chance of 'going for it'. The best BMX racers go for it unless they see it is too dangerous to do so, or they do not need to take the risk at that point of the competition. **You can use brake to help you get round berms for rear wheel drag or for sudden braking where you want to take an acute angle.**

*Top:* A world champion at work: England's own Mark 'Whoppa' Watkins.

*Above:* Notice the guy in front; he looks so relaxed.

## The big jumps (table tops, camels, King Kongs, Dolly Partons, etc.)

These are the jumps the spectators like, and so do the photographers. They make spectacular pictures and are very thrilling to ride, providing you have the right techniques.

There are no hard-and-fast rules for riding table tops or any variations to them. The only guidance that can be given is that the closer you stay to the surface the quicker you are going to be. I don't mean by this that you shouldn't jump them, but you mustn't get unnecessary air, because while you are floating you are not pedalling.

Unless you know a table top well, the decision as to how you hope to deal with it must be made in practice after you have developed a feel for it. Check the steepness (vert). Try a variety of approaches. Look at how some of the other riders are attacking it. By the time racing starts you should have it wired.

The power wheelie technique can come in handy on some table tops where there is a step-up. Lifting your front wheel up on to the ledge does away with the problem of impact. This means shifting your weight over the rear wheel, but once you hit the second ledge you must shift your weight back over the seat, otherwise you are going to bale out through the back end. If the vert on the second ledge sends you into orbit then you will need to transfer your weight back again over the rear wheel, because if you don't you have every chance of endoing!

In your practice sessions you should have perfected the technique of controlling the launching effect of the vert to a minimum because if you stay airborne for too long you will see other riders going past you.

**Top:** Where I like to be on the first berm.

**Above:** Gary Llewelyn (14), destined for the top. He was long gone when this pearler took place.

**Top left:** My city image; you have to pay attention to commerce if you are going to make BMX pay.

**Centre left:** This is for the crowd—not strictly racing technique.

**Bottom left:** I'm moving to the inside line here and closing it down for the Torker rider.

**Above:** Anthony Howells is out in front when it comes to the bends. He leans in and powers out.

**Opposite top:** This rider has moved away from his bike after the wipe-out, not a good thing to do; other riders can avoid a static target much more easily than a moving one.

***Above:*** Look at the concentration on that face!

## Air pedalling

The top American pros, and now some riders in the UK, have introduced the crazy technique of pedalling in the air. This may sound slightly stupid, but it isn't when you stop to think about it. Picture a long jumper when he is airborne. What does he do? Exactly—he runs in the air, and it gives him momentum! The same thing for the biker, except that there is an added reason for a BMXer to do it, and that is the take-up when the wheels first come into contact with the ground again! The bike rockets forward and there is no delay in the rider taking up his pedalling action again!

## Tracing the ground

Table tops which have a gap in them have been christened with a variety of names such as the King-Kong, the camel and, of course, a variety of water jumps. The idea is to jump the hole and, nine times out of ten, to use the vert on the face of the jump to clear the whole obstacle, which obviously is an absolute necessity when you are clearing a water jump.

Where there is firm ground in the recess some riders have developed a technique which takes the bike through in a line but traces the shape of the jump! The way in which this is done is to control the initial lift by pulling the bike up into the body, still pedalling, and to let it down in the channel, bringing it back up into the body for the final rim and setting down for traction on the back of the jump.

**Top left:** *This is John Vile (11) with Simon Bailey.*

**Centre left:** *Here's the Scottish nomad Andy Welsh. Believe it or not, this dude used to hitch-hike to meetings in England and he made a number 2 plate in UKBMX in 1984.*

**Left:** *Look at the first guy; a power wheelie to help him into the straight.*

## Drop-offs

This describes a jump where the ground suddenly falls away to nothing! They are OK when they are small, but there are some pretty diabolical drop-offs up and down the UK which have a height of 8 ft in some cases and fall away into a berm or a fast sweeper turn. One such track that has this feature is Birmingham Wheels, in the first straight down from the start hill. These are flyers whichever way you look at them, especially that one! You can't ride them any other way. The art is to get down to *terra firma* as fast as you can.

## Whoops

The word 'whoop' describes a multitude of jumps which range from the merest ripple to gigantic heaving mounds like the Dolly Partons at Poole (which I designed incidentally!). The Poole track has the two extremes in whoop design because in the final straight there is a set of low triples. Some people have said they thought the 'Dollys' were too dangerous, but I disagree because the rider has the choice of riding them or jumping them. If a rider has the skill and the nerve to jump them, there is no more spectacular a sight in BMX.

The smaller whoops at the end of the track demonstrate that it is not the size of the obstacles that presents the biggest problem, but the way in which they are spaced. The smaller triples at Poole bring just as many riders to grief as the Dolly Partons!

Very often, whether you are going to jump or ride a set of whoops depends on the speed you can achieve on the run in. With triples you can often ride the first one and get enough air to jump the other two, so this is worth considering as an option. Whenever you are riding whoops you should use the power wheelie technique and keep pedalling for as long as you can.

*Top right:* Here's one of my men, super-fast Anthony Howells (4505). Looks like he's got trouble here.

*Above centre:* Three riders taking the same line on the berm. The back rider swoops low here.

*Above:* You **have** to be tough!

49

# TRAINING TO WIN

BMX is no different from any other sport. If you want to be successful you have to train and train hard.

There does seem to be a naive belief among many young riders in the sport that as long as they just ride their bikes a few times a week they will be all right. This just isn't so! In order to improve at any sport which demands good physical condition, you have to improve your own physical capacity. The only way you can do that is to take yourself one step further in the amount of physical effort you can withstand.

I see training for the BMX rider as falling into four categories: track training on your BMX bike; ten speed training; weight training; aerobic activity for heart/lung development.

Whether or not all these methods are used depends on the age of the rider. For example, I would not advise anybody to use weights under the age of thirteen, and only a light weights/high repetitions programme even then.

Obviously the very young rider would not want to be out on the roads using a ten-speed racing bike, and it is very doubtful whether aerobic development over and above his BMX bike riding would serve any purpose whatsoever.

From the age of ten, depending on the size of the rider, I think ten-speed work is a good thing; and, for all age groups, regular track training is a must, and the most important part of a BMX rider's fitness and skill programme.

## Training on your BMX

The first requirement of any BMX rider who is serious about his sport is his own personal start gate. There are several good designs on the market but, failing one of these, you can easily knock up your own gate using two pieces of wood, hinges and a gate arm.

I do like to do about 60–70 starts each day, and I sometimes feel I ought to do more. Even if you are only a beginner you should be aiming at getting in about 20 starts daily.

## Geared for starting

In practice is the time to find out what gearing suits you for good starts. Experiment with different ratios. Work on different ways of keeping the start lights in vision, and of keeping other riders in view, while still keeping an eye on the track surface.

**Never do things in training that the rules won't allow you to do in a real race situation.** Any bad habits cultivated in training will put you at a disadvantage on race days, and when it comes to training on your starts, that means observing the lane rule out of the gate. Keep straight for at least 15 metres every time you do a practice start.

Practise balancing for much longer times than would ever be necessary at a proper race meeting. If it's a windy, blustery day, take advantage of these bad weather

*Any second now I'll push my weight forward and start pedalling!*

conditions to practise your balances in conditions you will often encounter on race days, especially in the UK.

When you use different gearings, change your crank positions to get the best from them. Remember, the lower the gearing the quicker you will get out of the gate, and the quicker you will pick up if it's a stop/start track. Remember, too, that you might run out of gas on a lower gearing if there are some long flat straights.

## Timing

If you do your training with a friend, try pitting each other's starts, to a given point, against the clock. It helps to have proof of improvement, if any is taking place.

## Start hill conditions

Try to use your practice start gate on an incline. You won't ever come across a start that is on the flat.

Have your friend give the start gate command, trying to follow the starter's cadence.

## Berm practice

You can use the clock in berm practice to real advantage. Start from a given spot and finish always at the same mark and take different lines round the berm. It will tell you the ideal way to berm when there aren't any riders impeding you. Experiment with braking techniques.

*Tim and Frankie Romain working at passes on the berm.*

*Balance: you need it under any conditions.*

Try riding with front and back brake. It stops you quicker and as a result you can pedal for longer. OK, so it's more weight, but you might find it's worth it. **Work at all your jumping techniques.**

## Stamina work on the BMX track

You have to work at your skills, your trackcraft, whenever you train with your BMX bike at the track, but you can also use the session to get some really heavy work in on the stamina side. BMX may be a sprint sport but, as anybody knows who's done it, you pretty soon run out of gas when you are being pushed by eight others who want to be where you are. It's very tiring too when you are chasing backsides!

## Interval training

Try sprinting the whole of the track and taking a five minute breather. Sprint it again, but this time take a four minute breather. Sprint it again, but the next time take a three minute breather, and so on, until your sixth and seventh sprints are consecutive; in other words, you do your last two circuits of the track together!

*This page: Gate training.*

## Road work on your BMX

First of all, make sure your bike is road legal—two brakes, reflectors, etc. At no time should you be attempting to beat speed records on a busy road. It is far too dangerous! So try to find a quiet road, but still you should not go mad. What you can do, though, on the roads is hill training. Find some pretty steep hills and work against them. You will build up your legs and your cardio-vascular system and you won't be doing the sort of speeds that constitute a danger to other road users and yourself.

## Ten speed training

More and more BMX riders are turning to their ten speeds to help them in their search for race fitness.

If you want to make your training pleasant there is no better way of doing it. Find some nice routes and get some miles in. If you don't have the time for long-distance work, then use your gears to make life hard for you over short distances.

## Weight training

If there is any one aspect of training that you can count on to cause controversy it is weight training. There are people in the sport who

are dead against it, and there are others who swear by it. What I'm saying is, it is a matter of your own personal instincts and feelings. If you reckon it makes you feel better and improves your performance, then—*do it!* If you don't then do the other thing! Personally, I think it is a really good way for the BMX ace to get fit and to improve performance. The reason I say this is that BMX is a total body sport. It isn't just about using one particular part of your body. You need the help of every muscle you can get. You especially rely on strength in the upper body and the finest way to develop that, I have found, is by using weights.

As I said earlier, weights are not for the very young and in the early teens they should only be used selectively, but past 14 I think they can accelerate fitness.

Squats with weights on the shoulders are very useful for developing thigh power, and presses, cleans and curls are great for the arms.

The middle part of the body is so important to a cyclist and, for that reason, you should work at sit-ups using weights. You must find the amount of weight you can comfortably manage at the outset and *gradually* build from that. Chins are good for middle body development.

Other work, but without weights, which is good for the legs is star jumps. These are done from a squat position, and you jump as high as you can aiming at the shape of a star. Squat thrusts are another good exercise and both of these are very effective in giving you greater stamina.

## Running

I personally don't like running and I feel it isn't good for the muscles you use as a rider, but it might be good for other people. I happen to know there are some top BMX people who do a lot of running and sprinting. If it suits you, do it, and you can be sure it is good for the engine room—the heart!

# TUNING YOUR BIKE

You can have the best bike in the world but if you don't look after it you might just as well race on a cheapie!

When it comes to tuning a racing car, a great deal of the mechanic's work goes into getting the engine finely balanced. You are the engine for your bike but you do have another 'engine room' on your bike, and that is the bottom bracket and cranking system. This is where we can start to get your bike in top racing order. You might be lucky and have a bike which has the very best in 'engine room' equipment, which means a sealed chrome–moly bracket, flight cranks and all chrome–moly spider and chainwheel. If you have, the only maintenance you will have to do is routine cleaning and tightening sessions after each outing.

If you are not so lucky and your units are not sealed, you are in for some arduous work.

After each race meeting you should strictly take your bottom bracket down, clean and re-grease it, checking that the races are all right and making sure you have removed all the dirt.

If the bottom bracket area is the engine room, the rear hub, freewheel and chain are the transmission. Here again, if you are not the owner of sealed units you must take it down regularly, re-grease and renew any worn or

*This Diamond Back Turbolite is a scrumptious machine, but it will be about as much use to you as a sack of wet spuds if you don't look after it!*

cracked bearings. **Check your chain all the time. It really can be the source of great misery and major pain if it lets you down at full grunt.** Use a good oil on your chain and carry a spare if you can.

Check for weak links and stretching. You can reduce the links where stretching occurs, but it isn't advisable because a certain amount of weakening must have taken place for this to happen. **Keep your chain clean. Give it a solvent bath after each meeting.**

## Wheels

Check them for buckles. If they are not straight get them straightened, or do it yourself if you are able.

Tune your spokes and look for any that are bent. Tighten them up evenly. Your front hub wants to run freely so give it a clean and re-grease it. Adjust the cones. Don't make them too tight. They will tighten a little when you clamp the locking nuts.

## Tyres

Tyres mean so much to the BMX

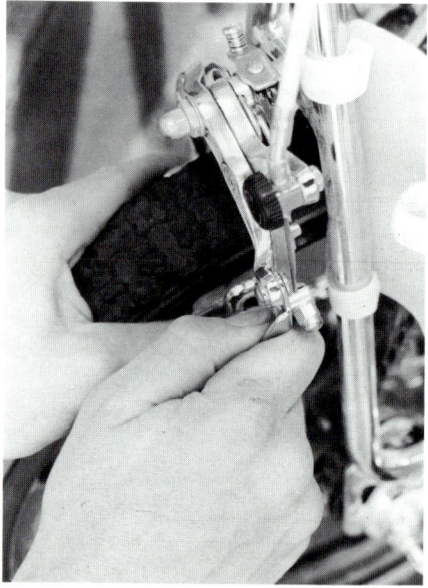

racer. They are ultra-crucial pieces of equipment and you neglect them at your peril!

Poor tyres will cause you to wheelspin, to slide out and to lose out in the traction stakes. You can't afford any of these things.

**Tread:** You need a good deep tread and you want the appropriate tread for the track you are riding.

An uneven, stony track needs tyres with a widely spaced tread so the stones can be absorbed and there is more rubber contact with the surface. If the track is smoother the tread can be closer and will give you more traction for this surface.

Check the walls for weakness,

usually revealed by a carbuncle or fraying.

**Keep your tyres clean:** Take a wire brush to meetings and get all the dirt, mud and grit out from between the knobbles. A tyre tread packed down with earth and stones will give you no grip whatsoever, and will not provide the flex needed to keep you upright on bends.

*Opposite left:* Making sure all is well in the headset department.

*Opposite right:* Getting the transmission link right; check your chain all the time.

*Opposite below left:* Chain wheel spider bolts must be done up tightly.

*Opposite below right:* Your brakes need to respond to the merest touch.

*Right:* This hasn't been seen on the BMX track before but I might try it!; note the elliptical chainwheel and the tensioner gear.

*Below:* Getting the rear wheel positioned correctly.

## Forks/headset

BMX bikes don't have any suspension, but they can still be smooth and generally are. You will know *how* smooth if you ever have to deal with a bike which has worn head bearings or bar stem/gooseneck. If any of these are worn, it will make a dance floor seem like the Rockies. You can check it out quite easily by standing astride your front wheel, clamping the tyre between your feet and lifting the bars. Any play will soon be obvious.

Keep the bearings in your headset well greased and clean and then the dreaded wear is less likely to happen.

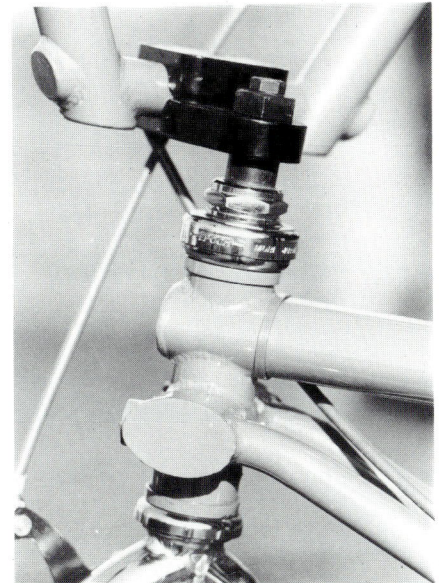

## Bar clamp

Make sure you have all the bolts fully tightened. Replace any worn bolts.

## Bar position

This is a crucial bit of your race tuning programme. Badly positioned bars can turn your whole day sour.

You cannot compensate for the wrong-sized frame by having your

*Left:* The head tube where stem and bearing wear can take place.

bars in an unnatural position. If you are a mini/midi rider, you want a bar position where the rise of your bars follows the same line as your head tube. If you are a bigger rider the rise of the bars wants to be straight.

## Brakes

Your brakes want to be responsive to the merest finger touch. That means having the proper adjustment on the cable, and having the lever in a position which makes it easy for you to operate. Keep the lever clamp tight.

**The caliper:** Check for good tension in your caliper spring. Replace it if it is worn because it will make your caliper off-centre all the time. To centralize your caliper, you can tap the spring on the side you want it to move with a centre punch. This usually does the trick.

**Brake blocks:** Keep them clean—there are special cleaners for the job. They aren't expensive so don't go racing with unevenly worn brake shoes.

# BMX STARS

It is a sign of the strength of BMX in the UK that already, after only five years, it has its own galaxy of well known stars.

There are few people in the UK, no matter what their sporting interest, who haven't heard of Andy Ruffell. Andy's fame as a BMXer has taken him into television and has made him a household name.

 I find myself often appearing on TV and being interviewed by national newspapers, and I must admit this is good for me, but it is also good for BMX that it has awakened such wide interest in the UK.

For the BMXers of the UK, the magical names they have grown up with are the American stars. When they visit the UK their life is one long round of signing autographs and answering thousands of questions for their many admirers. They deserve their adulation because they are at the top of their sport and they know how to treat their public; furthermore, they appreciate that without the fans and admirers they are nowhere.

Greatest showman of all the current American greats has to be Mike 'Hollywood' Miranda. He is a showman through and through, and is always so good with the youngsters. On top of that he is a great rider and has won many top honours in the USA and abroad.

Greg Hill is a name every BMXer knows, and he is a super pro in every sense. Greg has been the biggest single influence in my career since I had the pleasure and honour of staying at his home on one of my early visits to the USA. Greg represents everything a truly professional sportsman should be. He works hard in training at his sport, he works hard at the promotional side and on race days he gives his all to getting the very best out of himself.

Eric Rupe is another great American superstar and an amazing character. He doesn't look as if he has much power. He is small and not exactly endowed with that athletic look possessed by riders such as Brian Patterson and Greg Hill. Don't be fooled! This man is made of iron and he is fast, which is why he has won both association titles in the same year.

**Below:** Andy Ruffell in unfamiliar role as a freestyler—some air!

**Opposite:** A galaxy of American pros at a Paris meeting.

**Opposite top:** Out in front, Harvey Munkton; like Mike Miranda, he puts his successs down to God.

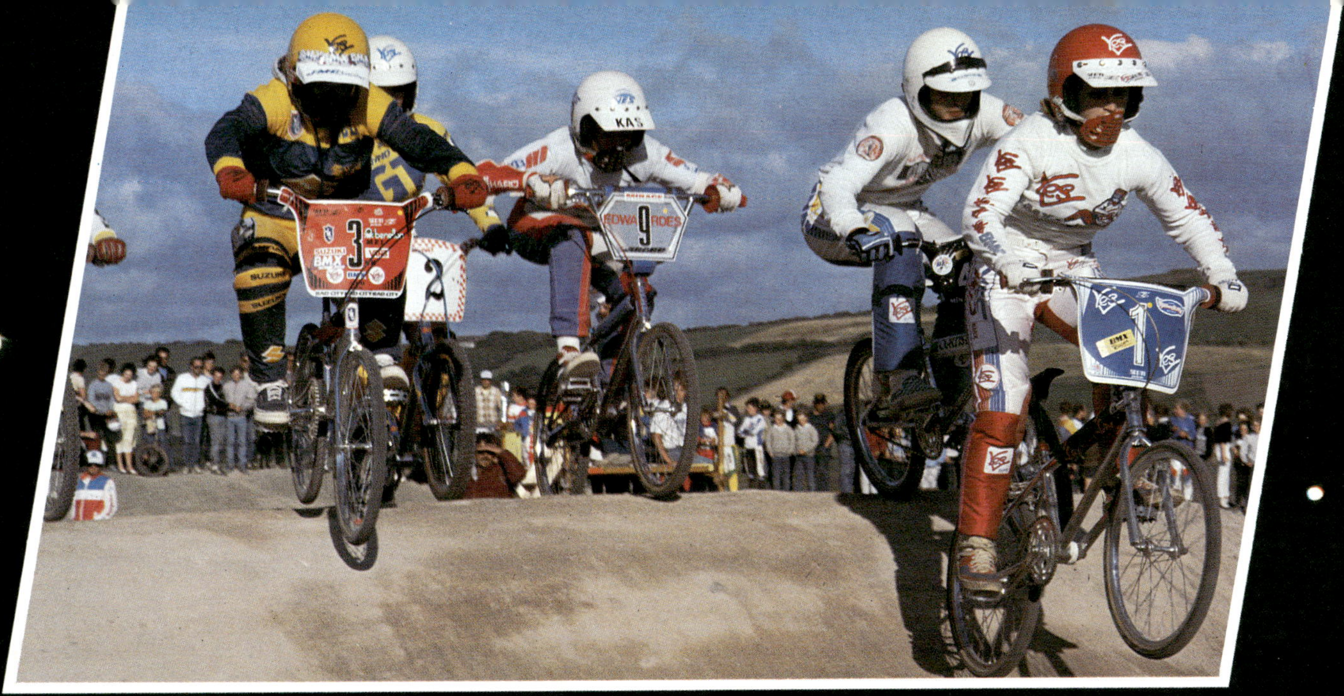
KAS
3
2
9
1
SUZUKI

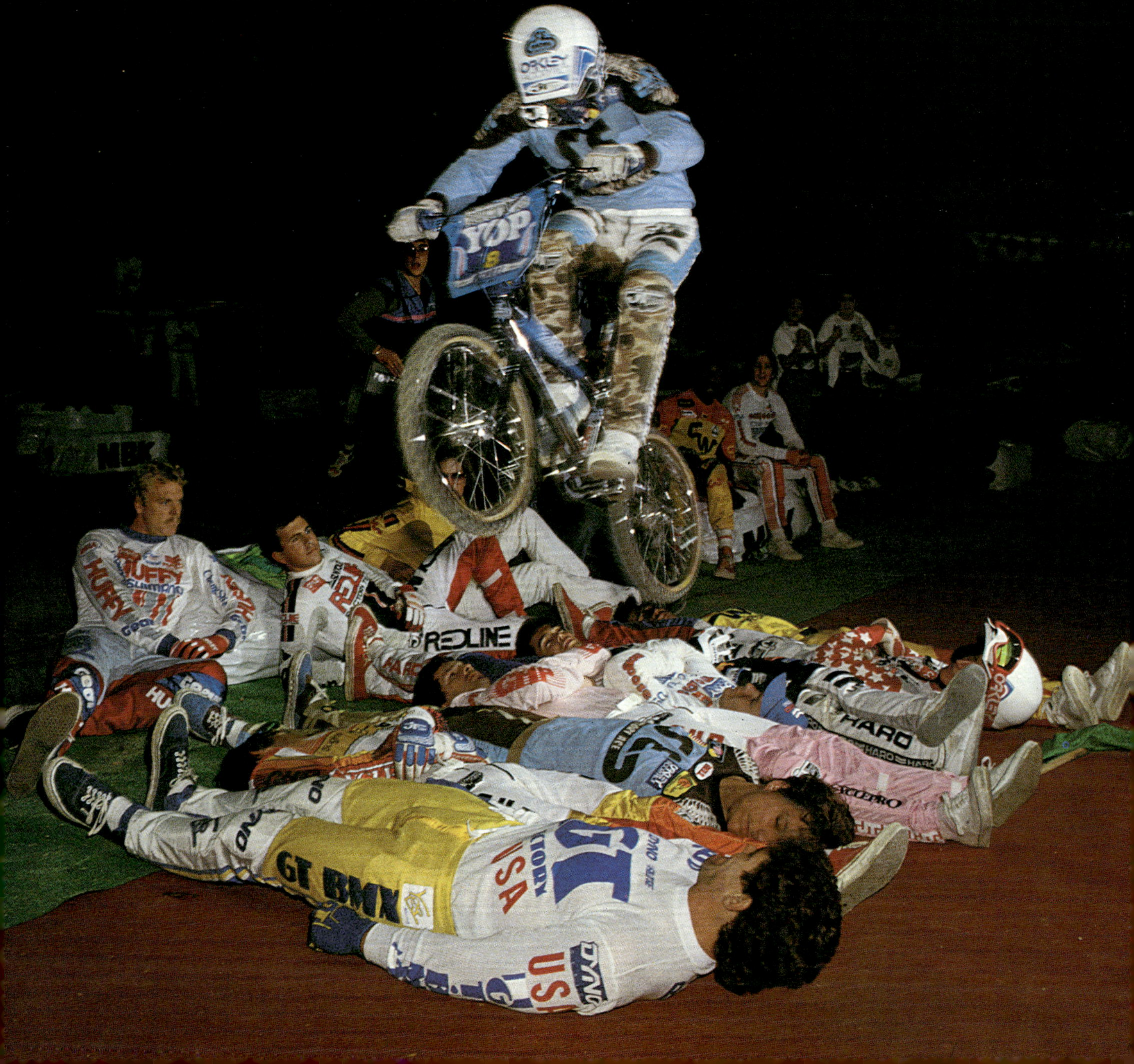
OAKLEY
YOP
REDLINE
HARO
GT BMX
USA
HUFFY

Stu Thompsen is a rider who has been at the top for a long while and he is like Greg Hill; he trains hard, and rides hard on race days.

Pete Loncarravich, whom I have had the honour of riding against in the UK, is another super-fit rider who has superb trackcraft and the C.W. man is never scared to put his reputation on the line against anybody!

We have a great American rider over in the UK at the moment by the name of Anthony Sewell. He has had a few back problems lately but in the past has won just about everything there is to win back in the USA, and he is giving the UK pros a hard time at the moment! Anthony is guesting for the Birmingham Wheels team.

There are so many brilliant riders in the USA that I could go on for a lot longer, but let's talk about some of the top riders we have in the UK and Europe.

I have spoken already of Andy Ruffell, who is one of BMX's established superstars; let me introduce you now to a relative newcomer, Geth Shooter, a rider you are going to hear a lot of in the future. This dude is dynamite! Geth made a name for himself in 1984 on the NBMXA circuit and moved into UKBMX towards the end of the season. It was immediately obvious that he had what it takes, and he backed it up in 1985 by turning pro straight away. He has done very well so far and with his ability will continue to do so. Geth rides for

Redline, and has made history by being the first English pro rider to win a pro-main against American riders. [Kellogs—May 1985]

Anybody who has been following BMX in the UK since it started will need no introduction to Pete Middleton, the Ammaco rider. Pete has been top rank for four years and is still one of the riders I have to fear all the time.

Ask any BMX follower who is the maddest of them all on the circuit, and they will tell you it is Mad Mark 'Sid' Salisbury. If anything wild or crazy is going to happen in a race, you can bet your life 'Sid' will be in the middle of it.

Another rider in the pro class you have to mention is big Trevor Robinson. Trev is a dedicated professional and works hard at his sport. He has recently changed sponsors and now rides in the colours of Halfords.

*Opposite top left:* Two of freestyle's greatest, R.L. Osborne and Eddie Fiola.

*Opposite bottom left:* Pete Middleton.

*Centre top:* Two top men duelling.

*Above:* Tim Judge, pro.

*Left:* Anthony Sewell battling it out with me at a European Superclass meeting.

**Top left:** Greg Hill, a great influence on me and a credit to BMX.

**Centre left:** Xavier Redios, top French rider and a great character.

**Bottom left:** Our very own Charlie Reynolds; Charlie is a big crowd pleaser and is never short of a gimmick!

**Opposite top:** Mike 'Hollywood' Miranda, a great showman and longtime pro with two American S.E. racers.

**Top:** On the inside, Clarence Perry, C.W. pro and a big powerful guy.

Of course, UK racing isn't centred around Pro-class racing; it involves every age group from five up to forty five. It involves girls, too, and there are plenty of them who would get the vote for star rating from many of the male riders!

In the lower age group there can be no better representative of the sport than David Maw, who rides in the seven year olds age group. David won the World Championship in 1984 in Japan for six year olds, and won every single race he went in for in the UK Nationals. What a record of consistency, and a nicer kid you couldn't wish to meet!

These mini dudes are great. We have a character in my team by the name of Colin Webb, and you should see the effort this kid puts into BMX. He is six and has taken some pretty hairy spills, but you just can't keep him down. Anthony Howells is another ace rider. He won the UK and the NBMXA twelve year old championships last year, and in the thirteens Wayne Llewelyn made number 1 UK and won the European title.

His brother Gary Llewelyn is another hot property and he is the UK No. 1, European No. 1, and in 1985 has established himself as a prime contender for the European Superclass crown.

Stu Diggens is another British household name, and this year has signed a big contract with Raleigh. He is having a few problems, but doubtless his ability will put him back at the top again. You cannot sign off from the older riders without mentioning that ace character Charlie Reynolds. He is the man who puts the fun into BMX. Others are Craig Schofield, who has been there since BMX started in the UK and Frankie Romain, a member of my team, who is one to watch for the top spot in the future.

A word about the girls, and the rider who has been top more than any other powder puff is Debbie Scott Webb. She is small but she is determined, and has held number 1 spot three years running. Before the new age groups came in, her greatest battles were always with Melanie Vauvelle, the glamour rider in the girls' class.

Hard to beat and a consistent winner is Sarah Jane Nichol. She is fast and is now riding Cruiser with the boys, or should I say against them! We compete a lot in Europe now and come up against top-class continental riders. Of these a few stand out, and top of the list must be Phil Hoogendoorn of The Netherlands and his fellow countryman Leon Walravens. These are both European champions. From France, François Lalli and Xavier Redios stick out.

*Centre:* Typical Charlie Reynolds. He came over a 'blind' ledge for this one and bought the farm 30ft down.

# BMX TEAMS

The diagram illustrates the structure of BMX sponsorship in the UK. There are a number of riders who have sponsorship but are not part of a team. Their support is on a small-scale or individual basis. The same usually applies to small product sponsorship. Rarely is a team linked to this, and most support of this kind is over and above existing team support and in the nature of co-sponsorship.

Recently the idea has taken root of private individuals, who do not have a direct BMX marketing spin-off, sponsoring quite large teams. Prime examples of this are the 1985 formation of Rainbow Racing and the Alan Sopp Racing team.

Small shops mostly sponsor individual riders, but there are exceptions such as the Edwardes team and Youngs. The largest shop combine team is Halfords, with anything up to a ten-man team. Quite often distributors' teams carry the name of the bike they ride, and

## THE BMX TEAM & SPONSORSHIP STRUCTURE

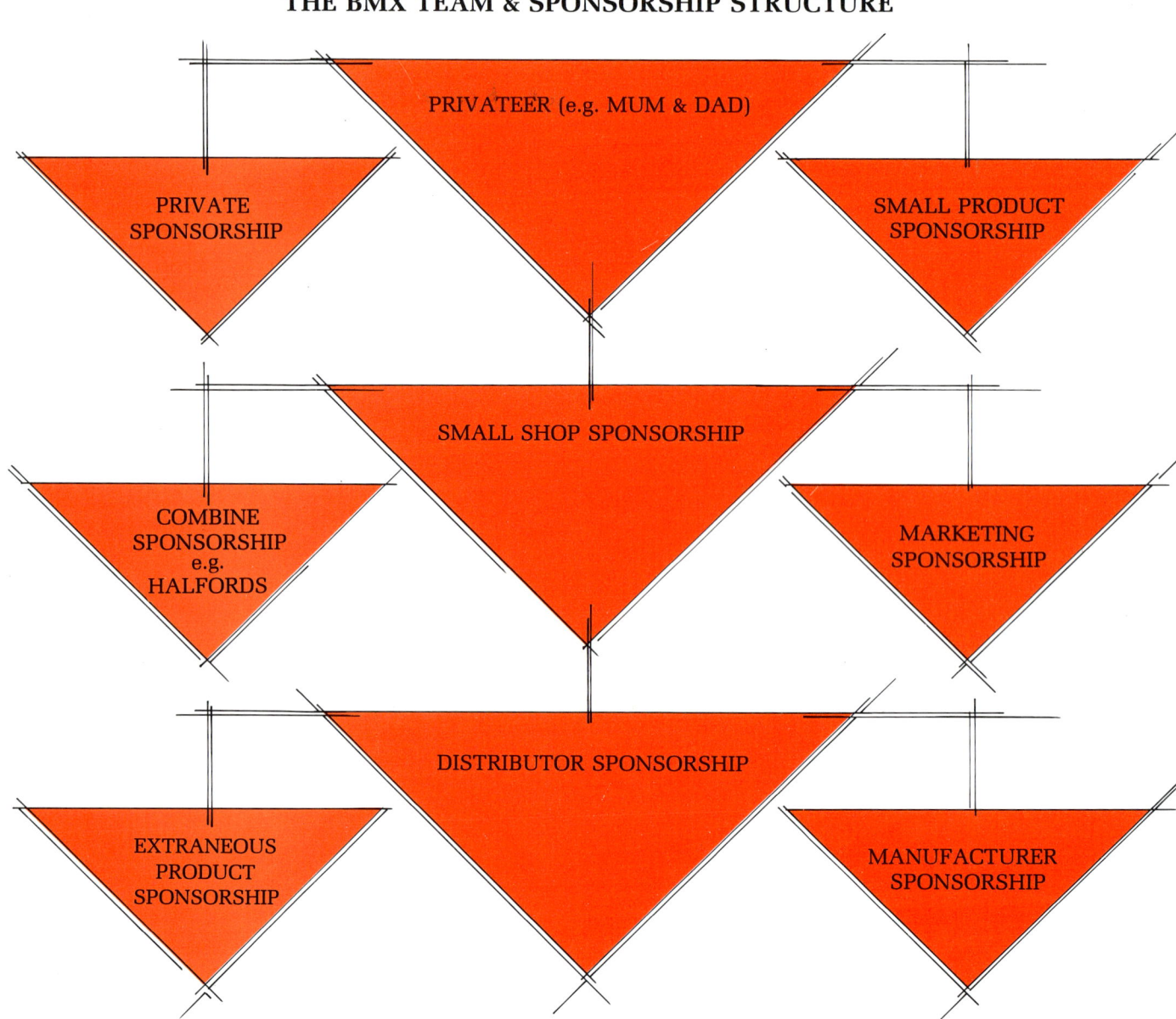

PRIVATEER (e.g. MUM & DAD)

PRIVATE SPONSORSHIP

SMALL PRODUCT SPONSORSHIP

SMALL SHOP SPONSORSHIP

COMBINE SPONSORSHIP e.g. HALFORDS

MARKETING SPONSORSHIP

DISTRIBUTOR SPONSORSHIP

EXTRANEOUS PRODUCT SPONSORSHIP

MANUFACTURER SPONSORSHIP

this is the case with the Diamond Back team, which is in fact backed by Freewheeler Leisure.

Bike teams such as Hutch and Redline are financed by the manufacturers but are run by distributors in the UK.

Marketing sponsorship is represented by people such as the YES organization who market a wide range of BMX and motorbike products.

My own team is quite unique in that it is run by a racer—*me!* I finance my team from the money I make endorsing products which are marketed by the Tran-Am organization. I also manufacture certain products. To help with costs I have co-sponsors and have, as an example of extraneous sponsorship, just completed a deal with VG, the food and grocery chain outlet.

Teams compete for a National championship and in 1985 March Racing won the Nike Trophy for the best team in the UK.

## Getting into a team or finding sponsorship

The question I am most asked by ambitious riders is, 'How can I get into a team', or, 'How can I get sponsorship'.

Basically, you have to work hard at your sport, do well and make the people who matter sit up and take notice. Having said this, there are a lot of very good riders who are not getting sponsorship.

*Craig Schofield, L.H. with the Raleigh team.*

Ask yourself why companies want to sponsor riders and you will be getting near to a solution. They have something to sell and they consider that if their products are linked or endorsed with your name they will sell better. It is as simple as that!

The next stage in the operation is to convince a company that this will happen if they support you. To do that you have to be getting good results and good publicity. If you are getting publicity you are a good part of the way there. Another point they will be interested in is your personality. They don't want their products associated with somebody who is rude, scruffy and a bad sport. They will want a rider who is none of these things and who has built up a good reputation. You need to remember this from the minute you start racing. It is no good suddenly becoming whiter than white when you realize you want sponsorship. You may already have forged an undesirable image which will take years to erase, and by the time yo have done that it will be too late. you think you are worth sponsorship (and you don't have to be a number 1 to think that) then get together a portfolio of yourself stating your experience, what you have won and competed in, any promotions or presentations you have done, and any pictures of you which have appeared anywhere in the media. Put it all together, and send it to any potential backers. Before you do so though, always

remember this: once you get backing, you have to keep going. There is no such thing as resting on your laurels in the business world, so make sure you think you are up to coping with the increased pressures!

**Left:** Here is a unique team—the Birmingham Wheels. This was formed for out-of-work kids in Birmingham and encompasses all 'wheel' sports.

**Above:** The English C.W. team and their American brothers on tour last year in the UK.

# FREESTYLE

The final leg of our journey along the BMX trail is freestyle. I am not a freestyler myself, but I am a great fan of freestyle. It is great fun, and so skilful, that you can't help but admire the riders who have mastered its many movements.

The great Bob Haro brought freestyle to the fore with some amazing tricks which, up to his arrival, weren't thought possible on a bike which wasn't fitted with any form of suspension.

He is a freestyle legend but now there are other great names to emerge from the USA, and we in the UK are breeding a brilliant kind of freestyler ourselves.

The big names to emerge from the USA are riders such as Eddie Fiola, R. L. Osborne, Michael J. Buff, Brian Wilkerson (who recently won the Kelloggs Frosties Freestyle Championship in Birmingham), Bryan Blyther and Brian Scura. In the UK we have the current king of the skateparks, Craig Campbell, and aerial king and world record holder Glyn Lewis. Eddie Preston and Mike Pardon are another two who are making a name for themselves, while my racing counterpart, Andy Ruffell's brother Neil, is cutting an exciting path to the top and he put on a fantastic show at the Kelloggs by making the two-man final against Brian Wilkerson. He lost, but to get there he had better scores than the king of freestyle, Eddie Fiol.

Where does racing end and freestyle begin? This is Craig Schofield getting flat and high.

*Left:* Gymnastic shapes and dance are becoming more important in competition freestyle; this is D.P. factory rider Trevor Cowell showing how.

*Below left:* Charlie Reynolds is a racer but he's so wild he just has to get air wherever he goes. He's working at his freestyle.

Freestyle developed in the skateparks as the skateboard phenomenon waned. That is where Haro did a lot of his experimentation, and of course the ramps, such as the quarter and half pipes and the trick ramps, are mobile reconstructions of the facilities offered by the skateparks.

Since those early days in the 1970s, things have progressed along more organized lines with proper competitions, championships and schemes for grading the ability of individual exponents. In the UK now, the UKBMX association has its own freestyle wing and a licence is needed to be able to compete in competitions sponsored by that association.

Freestyle has caught on with the media; several competitions, displays and interviews have been screened on TV and the press have been quick to cover any freestyle venues which are more of a stunt nature, such as car jumping or river jumping.

'Getting air' is one of the most sensational freestyle moves. A rider gets air off a quarter pipe or in the Performance Bowl of a skatepark.

The rider takes a run at the ramp, which is shaped like a quarter of a circle, and the shape of the surface projects him and his bike into the

air! The world record for air achieved above the lip of the quarter pipe is held by Glyn Lewis of England, with a height of over six foot.

In competitions the excellence of an aerial isn't necessarily judged by height, but by the style and variations a rider can put into his repertoire. There are look back, cross-up, one handers, one hander-no footers and table-top aerials.

The quarter pipe is a very versatile piece of equipment and many other freestyle moves can be performed on it. Here are a few.

## Quarter-pipe freestyle

**Foot plant:** The rider plants one foot at the top of the pipe when he is actually above his bike and hanging out from the pipe at right-angles. It is most spectacular when done in a Performance Bowl because the drop to the bottom of the bowl is a long one if anything goes wrong.

**Pop-out:** The rider goes up the curve of the pipe and jumps off his bike on to the platform at the top of the pipe.

**Drop-in:** Once the rider is standing on the platform he holds his bike upright on the rear wheel, puts one foot on a pedal and drops into the curve of the pipe and rides out.

**Backward drop-in:** Not many riders can do this one. One of its better exponents is Woody Itson from the USA. The rider has his back to the curve of the pipe and performs an endo on his front wheel with the rear wheel hanging out over the lip. He then lets the rear wheel drop into the curve of the pipe and rides out backwards.

**Opposite:** Hot air and wild antics from this S.E. racer meddling in the freestyle scene!

**Right:** A. Ruffell freestyle show at the Sobell.

**Mounted pop-out with a balanced landing:** This is the same as a pop-out except that the rider does not get off his bike. He actually flies off the lip of the pipe, turns his bike sideways and lands on both wheels without either foot touching the ground.

**Mounted drop-in:** Having held his balance, the rider hops the bike to the rim of the platform and drops into the curve of the pipe, turning the bike to the front at the last moment so he can ride down and out.

Neil Ruffell again: you can't keep this ace down!

71

**Foot plant above the quarter pipe:**
The quarter pipe needs to be against a wall. The rider gets as much air as he can but, instead of pulling his bike out so he can link with the parabola of the pipe, he lets the vert of the pipe take him up in a straight line. He then sticks his foot out to plant it on the wall, turning his bike underneath him as he does so. Now he drops into the curve of the pipe and rides out.

These are some of the more advanced quarter pipe moves the freestyler does but, of course, there are many less demanding ones such as rollbacks, where the rider just rides up the pipe and rolls backwards down it. These are the types of trick it is wise for the beginner to attempt to start with. The quarter pipe is a spectacular piece of equipment, but the trick ramp, which is much smaller, does provide a setting for some very impressive freestyle work.

*A pretty bulky head tube hung with trick componentry; the platforms are used for moves.*

*Andy Ruffell made his name as a racer, but he's a pretty hot freestyler too.*

## The most popular moves on the trick ramp

**The rampstall:** The rider rolls up the ramp pulling a wheelie as he goes. He takes the rear wheel right to the edge of the ramp before stopping and hopping back. He then rolls out backwards. A neat way of finishing any rollback move off a ramp is with a slider. To do this you have to pull the bars round just over 90° and slide the bike round on the front wheel, before riding out frontways.

**Kick turns:** This is a 180° spin at the top of the trick ramp. The rider rolls up the ramp at medium pace, brakes and spins pushing the wheel down when he has completed the 180° turn and riding out.

There are variations to this and they are as follows.

**The one-hand one-footer kick turn:** The same thing except the rider takes one hand off the bars and one foot off the pedals. The more gymnastic the pose the better the trick looks!

**Touch the front wheel kick turn:** The rider takes one hand off the bars and touches the front wheel with it.

**Peak salute kick turn:** The rider takes one hand off the bars and touches the peak of his lid with it.

**Cross-up kick turn:** The rider, as he makes the 180° turn, crosses the bars up 180° and uncrosses them by the time the wheel touches down on the ramp.

**Ramp endo:** Ride up the ramp and apply the front brake at the top, shifting body weight to the front of the bike. Hold the position for as long as possible and then roll back.

**Front wheel 180°:** Roll up the ramp as for the endo and begin to twist in the direction you have chosen. The rear wheel comes round above the lip of the ramp, but you must release the brake before the moment of touchdown comes, otherwise you are about to take a trip over the back of the ramp.

**Front wheel 360°:** This is a radical

*This is Simon Kefford; his father is the UKBMX supremo. He's got style, this dude!*

move and you had better know what you are doing! Move up the ramp as you did for the 180°, apply the front brake and start the spin. The difference with this one is that you are riding into the ramp and coming out of it backwards. At the point of making 180°, your weight should have shifted to the front of the bike and will now gradually shift backwards over the seat for the rollback.

**The 540° kick turn:** Now we are talking ace moves. It starts off as a kickturn and you have to spin a 360° and then the other 180° to bring yourself to the ride-out position. When you initiate the first spin you move your body weight up as close to the bars as you can and you keep it there until you are nearly through with the final 180°.

## Groundwork

A lot of freestyle is done on the ground and very skilful much of it is too. This is where most of the kids start to get their freestyle act

together in the streets or on any piece of waste land. There is so much you can do with this kind of freestyle, and all you need is your bike and a bit of determination. Most kids start with this one:

**The bunny-hop:** Just a straightforward case of riding at an obstacle and lifting your bike over it. Start low and work up.

**Pogos (back wheel hops):** You could call this a bouncing wheelie. You pull a wheelie and hold it very high and bounce your bike on the back wheel.

**Front wheel hops:** A lot harder than the others and, before you attempt it, you need to be an endo specialist. You need a good front brake. Pull it on. Push your weight forward over the bars and hold a balance. Now start hopping by pulling on the bars.

**Kerb endo:** Ride slowly into the kerb, pull the front brake, shift your weight forward and let the back come up. Hold the balance.

**Rockwalk:** Ride in. Apply the front brake. Move your weight to the side

you want to spin and push the back wheel round 180°. Once it touches down, pull a wheelie and lift the front wheel round another 180°.

**Broncos:** This is the one where you transfer from front wheel hops to pogos.

**Front wheel 180s and 360s:** Same as on the trick ramp, but you do it on the ground. Ride in, apply the front brake, shift your weight to the side you want to spin, and rotate the rear of the bike round.

There are many others, and you will find them in specialist freestyle books. Enjoy the ride!

## The freestyle bike

The freestyle bike is a different animal from the racing bike, and if you are going to get serious about freestyle you will need the proper machine. Apart from being able to do more freestyle on a proper bike

*Living on the edge. Paul Hudson balancing on the rim of a Performance Bowl; it's a long way down if he goofs it!*

**Opposite:** Neil Ruffell showing why he's moving to the top of the freestyle world.

**Left:** This dude is Jess Dyrenforth and he is another of the brilliant UK freestylers to emerge in the last year.

**Below:** Craig Campbell, trackstanding on the lip of the bowl.

**Opposite top:** Glyn Lewis showing why he holds the world aerial record.

you will be safer if anything goes wrong, because bike manufacturers are unwilling to back their guarantees if a racer is used for freestyle.

**The difference between a freestyle and a racing bike:** The first noticeable difference is the weight. Freestylers aren't as weight-conscious as racers, and usually the freestyle bike is anywhere between the 26 and 30+ lb mark. The reason for this is the size of tube used to get

the necessary strength, the beefiness of the drop-outs, the coaster brake, the mag wheels, two caliper brakes and various other appendages which the rider needs to go through his range of moves, such as front and rear platforms (sometimes known as pegs), triple top tubes for standing tricks and platform overhangs behind the seat.

**The coaster brake:** Top freestylers like to work with these, because it gives them instant control for making speed adjustments and tricks such as kickturns. They fit into the rear wheel and operate off the pedals; they take some getting used to.

**Triple top tube:** Two smaller-gauge tubes run alongside the main top tube to give a better balancing platform for moves like the surfer (a standing balance while the bike is in motion.)

**Back platform:** This is an overhang behind the seat and above the rear brake caliper. Some riders use it for standing tricks, and is used for to stand on for one-hand one-footer kickturns.

**Front fork stunt pegs:** These are either extra-long front wheel nuts, or they are built into the front forks. They are used for balance tricks, front wheel hops and for walking moves such as the reverse thrust (where the rider walks round his bike).

# BMX DICTIONARY

**Ace:** Excellent, top; BMX star
**Ankle biter:** Young BMXer/mini dude
**Armour:** Plastic protective clothing

**Bad:** Good, cool, ace
**Baking cakes:** Flying, stoking, speeding
**Banzai:** Going for it
**Bear trap:** Vicious-looking pedal
**Beater:** A bike you thrash
**Berm:** A banked turn
**Berm warfare:** Hot action on the berms, any hot BMX action
**Biff:** To crash
**Bite it:** Bite the dust, crash, wipe out
**Blasted:** Beaten
**Blazing:** Speeding, hooking, cooking
**Block pass:** A pass on the berm where the rider comes wide and cuts across low
**Blow the doors off:** Great start
**Bodge:** Bottom bracket
**Bogus:** Not right, unfair, out of order
**Bongo:** Bad crash
**Boogie:** Go fast
**Boogie with the birds:** Get air
**Booning:** Ride out
**Bottom bracket:** Crank bearing housing
**Bought the farm:** Crashed
**Bozo:** Squid, dumbo
**Bunny-hop:** Freestyle jump over obstacle

**Cadence:** Starter's sequence
**Café racer:** Street bike
**Caliper:** Brake assembly on forks
**Camel:** Table top with humps
**Chrome–moly:** Chrome–molybdenum alloy steel

**Chew:** Buy it, crash
**Cinder chewer:** Rider prone to crashes
**Circling the drain:** Cancelling racing or training
**Coast:** Freewheel
**Coaster:** Hub brake
**Compo:** Racers in your class
**Cooking:** Moving fast
**Cool:** Hot, trick
**Cosmo:** Class, trick, cool
**Crank rank:** Start line-up
**Critical:** Going all the way
**Cross-up:** Turning bars fully in mid-air
**Cruiser:** Bike with 24 in. or 26 in. wheels

**Decal:** Sticker
**De-tuned:** Off form
**Dialled in:** Finely tuned
**Dogs:** Feet
**Double:** To win two classes at one event or to win two associations' championships
**Draft:** Use slipstream
**Drive train:** Transmission
**Drop-off:** Where ground falls away from jump
**Drop-out:** Slot in forks for axle
**Dude:** Rider
**Dumbo:** Bozo, squid, nurd
**Dyno rhino:** Good stuff, neat

**Eating dookie:** Crash badly
**Eating yoghurt:** Making a mess of a track or move
**Eat it:** Bite the dust, swallow dirt
**Endo:** Going over the bars; or, in freestyle, to balance on the front wheel

**Face guard:** Helmet protection for the nose and mouth
**Factory:** Trick, top gear, the ultimate equipment
**Factory ride:** Full sponsorship
**Far out:** The best, great
**Floval:** Aerodynamic shape, especially tubing
**Flute:** Groove for lightness
**Fly:** Go fast, jump
**Fruit loops:** Weird, refers to oddball
**Full grunt:** Maximum effort
**Full tilt bozo:** Going for it, but crazy
**Full toot:** Going as fast as you can

**Gate:** To start, the start gate
**Gator:** Gaiter, lower-leg protector
**Gnarly:** Hot, fast, scary, cool, trick
**Go!mobile:** Fast bike
**Goose-neck:** Handlebar stem with forward clamp
**Grab air:** Go into orbit
**Grind:** Eat
**Gussett:** Reinforcing plate in frame

**Heavy duty:** Neat stuff
**Hectic:** Good and wild
**Heli-arc:** Good quality welding
**Helicopter:** 180° turn of the bars in orbit
**Henderson:** A one hand, one footer with arm and leg fully extended
**Holeshot:** The lead out of the gate and inside position
**Honking:** Big
**Hooking it on:** Flying, speeding
**Hot:** Cool
**Hot licks:** Hot moves on a track
**Humming bird brains/alligator mouths:** Our competitors

**Immo:** Imitation
**Insane:** Wild, radical, lots of go
**Intense:** Total concentration

**Jam:** Go fast
**Jeez, Louise:** Exclamatory phrase
**Jersey sponsored:** Backing with a jersey and a discount, first time sponsorship

**Kamikaze:** Crazy, going for it!
**Kicking booty:** Winning, taking the spoils
**Klutz:** Worse than a bonzo, a nurd and a squid
**Knobbly:** Chunky tyre

**Lay back:** Seat that is bent to lengthen the frame
**Lame:** Weak, crummy, useless
**Latered:** Write off, wrecked
**Leary:** A jump with the rear wheel totally kicked out and the bars helicoptered
**Lid:** Crash helmet

**Main:** The final moto for trophies
**Max:** Maximum
**Mean motor scooter:** A speeder
**Mega:** Ultra, great, huge
**Mini:** Small BMX bike
**Motion lotion:** Oil, grease
**Moto:** Qualifying heat
**Moto sheet:** List of riders in a moto

**Neato jet:** Cool, neat
**Not receiving all his stations:** Not all there
**Novocain:** To blow away the opposition
**Nurd:** Likeable nutcase
**Nurdette:** Female likeable nutcase

**O.T.B.:** Over the bars

**Pearled:** Blitzed, bombed
**Perfect:** When a rider goes through the card, wins everything on the day
**Pizza elbows:** Result of crashing without sliders
**Plate:** Number plate
**Powder puff:** Female rider
**Pro bar:** Wide handlebar
**Pro section:** Most challenging section of the track
**Push:** To use a high gear

**Qual:** Top class
**Quarter pipe:** Curved freestyle ramp

**Radical:** Mad, stupendous, wild, outrageous
**Rear end:** Back of the bike
**Roost:** To chuck dirt up from a slide
**Rubber:** Tyre

**Sano:** Clean, well kept
**Scrutineer:** Bike inspector at race meetings
**Shindentation:** Result of pedal slip
**Sidehack:** BMX bike with a sidecar
**Sign-up:** Entry at a race meeting
**Skinny:** Light tyre
**Skoot:** A bike
**Slider:** Arm protector
**Slingshot:** Speed obtained from coming high off a berm
**Smoking:** Speeding
**Soil sample:** To crash and swallow earth
**Speed jump:** Small mound on track
**Spider:** Chainwheel centre
**Spin:** Use a low gear, pedal fast
**Splat test:** To thrash a bike
**Sprocket:** Freewheel
**Stuff:** To push somebody over a berm on purpose
**Stutter bumps:** Small bumps on a track
**Suicide hill:** The start hill
**Superqual:** The best
**Sweeper:** Unbanked bend
**Swoop:** To pass someone in a turn

**Table top:** A large jump named because it made riders flatten out their bikes in the air
**Tanker:** Cruiser
**Thrasher:** Bike used mostly for thrashing
**TIG:** Top quality welding technique (tungsten inert gas)
**Triple:** To win all three motos
**Tombstoned:** To put another rider in the dust
**Trash canned:** Totally destroyed
**Trick:** Hot equipment
**Trickenometry:** Advance study of trickology
**Twanged:** Accidentally reshaping a part on your bike

**Under the gun:** Under pressure
**Unreal:** Far out, unbelievable

**Whooper:** One in a series of whoops
**Wrecktangle:** Tangle of crash victims

**Zeroed:** Annihilated